Listen to People

Listen to People

John Tyndall

First Edition

Hidden Brook Press
www.HiddenBrookPress.com
writers@HiddenBrookPress.com

Copyright © 2020 Hidden Brook Press
Copyright © 2020 John Tyndall

All rights for poems revert to the author. All rights for book, layout and design remain with Hidden Brook Press. No part of this book may be reproduced except by a reviewer who may quote brief passages in a review. The use of any part of this publication reproduced, transmitted in any form or by any means, electronic, mechanical, photocopied, recorded or otherwise stored in a retrieval system without prior written consent of the publisher is an infringement of the copyright law.

Listen to People
John Tyndall

Editor – John B. Lee
Cover Design – Richard M. Grove
Cover Image – Michael-John Idzerda
Author Photo – David Murphy
Layout and Design – Richard M. Grove

Typeset in Garamond
Printed and bound in Canada and USA
Distributed in USA by Ingram,
      in Canada by Hidden Brook Distribution

Library and Archives Canada Cataloguing in Publication

Title: Listen to people / John Tyndall.
Names: Tyndall, John, 1951- author.
Description: First edition. | Poems.
Identifiers: Canadiana 20200254146 | ISBN 9781989786031 (softcover)
Classification: LCC PS8589.Y5 L57 2020 | DDC C811/.54—dc23

Dedicated with love to
Diane.

Contents

Lots of Love

– White Oxfords – *p. 2*
– The Tester – *p. 4*
– Falling Down: Father Tells Us – *p. 6*
– Wiarton Cenotaph: Father Tells Us – *p. 8*
– The Very Moment (2) – *p. 11*
– Highholder – *p. 12*
– Miscreant – *p. 13*
– Keepers – *p. 14*
– She Danced Before She Could Talk – *p. 16*
– Snow Crones – *p. 17*
– Ode to an Uncle – *p. 18*
– *Mind How You Go* – *p. 20*
– *For All Time Lamenting* – *p. 22*
– *Hear That?* – *p. 24*
– Gordon (Joe) – *p. 25*

Undetermined Significance

– *Boys, Are You Buzzing?* – *p. 28*
– MGUS GUMS SMUG MUGS – *p. 29*
– How She Knew Me – *p. 32*
– to Dance – *p. 34*
– EMG us – *p. 36*
– Kappa Lambda – *p. 38*
– Blood Work – *p. 40*
– Farewell Angelika – *p. 42*
– Tarnished Lining – *p. 44*
– FX-rays – *p. 46*
– Blet – *p. 48*
– *Praesagia mortis* – *p. 49*
– Creative Compensation – *p. 50*
– Undetermined Significance – *p. 52*
– *Go Ahead John* – *p. 54*

Listen

— Everything I Know about Library Science I Learned from The Kenny Burrell Quartet – *p. 58*
— The Archer and the Ugly Tourist – *p. 60*
— Tattered – *p. 62*
— Zsuzsánna is in Love Forever – *p. 63*
— *Sit Back and Listen* – *p. 64*
— Only a Dream Camino – *p. 66*
— Raven Plays the Mountain – *p. 68*
— The First Time Alice Munro Asked Me a Question – *p. 69*
— Take Up What You Hear – *p. 70*
— In the Wheelhouse – *p. 71*
— Two Paths – *p. 72*
— Himselven (ghazal) – *p. 73*
— Stars, the Stars – *p. 74*
— Moniker, Handle, Tag – *p. 75*
— Haunt – *p. 76*

Acknowledgements – *p. 79*
Author Bio – *p. 81*

You need to listen to people.

Margaret Avison, in conversation.

Lots of Love

White Oxfords

The last time I saw
my father alive
he was pilgrim
through his ninety years
sheltering under
Dover radar station
from German shelling
with women operators
and a bottle of whisky
he looked in my eyes
and warned *You've got
to return home now*
then he threw off
his hospital gown
and shouted *Get me
my white oxfords*
dressing late for a dance
somewhere during
the Great Depression

Sometimes he'd
react that way
to sedatives
other nights he'd
wonder at Bluebirds
perching on his toes
gaze at car-light
flowing upon the ceiling
like rainfall on glass
be mesmerized by red
smoke-detector flash
like an ambulance signal
and sometimes he'd
wake up clear-sighted
and ask for
a clean shave

The last time I
saw my father
his eyes had been
shut an hour already
although his mouth
gaped open
so I cupped his
still-warm chin
in my hand
trying to close it
but of course
the jaw fell again
and when his lips
parted they made
the minute sound
I'd heard countless
times just before
he'd begin to speak
saying perhaps his
signature *Goodbye
Lots of love*

The Tester

Flip the latches open
on the tube tester's hard lid
and you reveal
the switches
the varied plug-ins
the calibrated meter
with its swinging needle
the rolling selector
of vacuum-tube numbers
6B10, 6H6
12BE6, 12BY7A
and to a young boy
the mysterious light
leakage
spins tales of espionage
and it's an attaché case
preserving the first, second
and third worlds
from total nuclear
annihilation
or better yet
it's an alien device
hurtling its lord
across space and time
to save, well
EVERYTHING

But step aside, kid
this baby awaits
its real master
your dad, the electrician
knows what it's capable of
knows where to insert
a triode, a tetrode, a pentode
how to read the plate current
the screen grid signs
when to conduct
an emission test
a transconductance test
why to measure that tricky
interelectrode leakage
all the latest post-war
technologies at his command
so the short-wave radio
reaches Nancy, Rennes, Berlin-Ost
so the newfangled television
brings in CKLW, CBC
channel 9 to the universe
with his expert fingers
on its bakelite controls
your dad becomes part of
hell, he IS
the tube tester

Falling Down: Father Tells Us

Your great-great-uncle
Black Jack Tyndall
was an innkeeper
over in Lion's Head
and after serving customers
in his pub, serving them
and drinking himself
falling-down drunk
he'd be laid in his wagon
and his horse would trot
all the way home
where his family carried
him inside to sleep, stowed
the cart, bedded down the gelding
night after night

I hitched a horse like that
to a milk wagon on my route
through Wiarton in the thirties
a mare named Fly
and if I'd been out till dawn
dancing and drinking
she'd stop at every house
where I'd come around
long enough to deliver
milk and cream or buttermilk
and then stumble back
when she'd amble on
to the next customer
and the next until
our rounds were finished
and she would lope on back
to her stable at the creamery
so she kept me from falling
down on the job and getting fired
until one night at the movies
a guy came down the aisle
to tell me another horse
had kicked Fly, broke her leg
and did I want to be
the one who shot her

Wiarton Cenotaph: Father Tells Us

J. Patterson
    was James Patterson
    a tattooed infantryman
    we hooked up at Hastings
    and off we go to the pub
    where he'd pawned his fiddle
    to pay for his drinks
    they'd let him play it
    and give it back closing time
    so we had some pints
    and he fiddled and fiddled
    while the pub's parrot
    squawked and swore on the bar
    and it bit James's finger
    when he pointed at the bird
    and I never saw him again
    afterwards I heard tell
    he fought and died at Dieppe
    and I've always wondered
    what happened to his fiddle

R. Moore
    was Russell Moore
    we'd been schoolmates
    and he'd played piano
    for singing and dancing
    once at Hill of Ulbster
    radar station he stayed
    for a visit, shooting
    the shit and drinking
    and when he flew off
    we tracked his plane down
    the east coast of Scotland
    until he journeyed beyond
    our range and crashed
    on a foggy mountain
    Russell was buried over there
    but I brought back
    a snap of the grave
    his family couldn't visit

D. Wright
was Donald Wright
who lived across Taylor Street
from our old house
he wanted to enlist
in the merchant navy
and I got the address
so he could join up
and on his second trip
on this oil tanker
she was coming back
empty not washed out
when the torpedo struck
igniting the lingering gases
so she exploded
and Donald sank with her

The Very Moment (2)

In April 1918
the Great War not over
the Spanish Flu unknown
my grandmother
pregnant with my father
rode horse and buggy
and covered coach south
for seventy miles
through Bruce County
from Dyer's Bay, her home
in Lindsay Township
on cold Georgian Bay
to her sister's farmhouse
in Elderslie Township
where she bore
in warm company
her little Guy
on Tuesday, the 23rd

On Wednesday, the 7th
of January 2009
my love and I
raced north from London
through snowstorms
hoping in vain
to reach my dad's bedside
at Wiarton Hospital
while he still lived
yet at the very moment
he died alone
we drove past the place
of his birth

Highholder

Father, when I think of you
and the kingdom of birds
yes, I think of your beloved
Bluebirds and Tree Swallows
all those boxes you built
cleaned out and repaired
all those tears you shed
over stiff wee bodies
from a late Spring freeze
but most of all I hear you
exclaim *Highholder!*
at the rhythmic cry
Flicker-flicker-flicker
of *Colaptes auratus*
the Northern Flicker
an ant-eater, a lover of ants
digging in the sand
for a larval meal
outside your cottage
and you, a hater of ants
stomping two-footed
swatting two-fisted
hundreds of black pismires
inside your cottage
then vacuuming them up neat
as a Highholder's tongue
I think of you, Father
when I see its white rump
in flight through woods
a white as shining
as the box of your ashes

but you are not resting
in a grave at Balsam Grove
you are squawking *Yuck Yuck*
flying away, away, up, and up
to your high hole

Miscreant

On my mother's
side of the family
great-great-great-grandfather
Ludwig Wideman
fought with General Brock
during the War of 1812
but ended up dead
shot through the head
in the Rebellion of 1837
a supporter
of William Lyon Mackenzie
and a non-believer
in the Family Compact

On my father's
side of the family
great-grandmother
Mary Tyndall
was born Mary Christian
on the Isle of Man
a cousin of scoundrel
Mr. Fletcher Christian
who had no trust
in the justice
of His Majesty's
Royal Navy

Although there is no one
I would set adrift
upon the salt sea

sometimes

I think wicked thoughts
sense vile feelings
revel in the hereditable pacts
of blood and bone
                Hissst

Whom shall we overthrow
tonight

Keepers

For years my father
urged me to discover
Jones Falls, boyhood
playground for him
while visiting his
Springmount relatives

I had to hear
the cataract
feel the spray
close-up

Pouring
over the escarpment
skirting
immense boulders
broken off
rolled smooth
by glacial ice
the snowmelt-
thunderstorm-
rain-shower
Pottawatomi River
named for Keepers
of Sacred Fire
flows around a crag
and roars away

Now in Summer heat
my love and I hike
to the waterfall
where above the plunge
she can cross
smooth streambed
careful
as a white egret

We climb to the brink
over cedar roots
upon limestone layers
slippery snakes
and ladders
to watch time descend
beyond our lives

I must tell our son
to play here where
many bloodlines
have played

and become one
of the keepers
of flames and wind
and sand and falls

She Danced Before She Could Talk

For years one, two, three
Diane's inflamed ears
blocked the finer sounds
only the rhythms of speech
of music came through
membranes of pressure
spikes of pain
but while she murmured
in her own private language
she whirled and waltzed
she swayed and rocked
with all the joy of heart
in the face of suffering
till hot oil was poured in
to burst and to drain
the infected canals
and as words finally
seeped deep within her
so then speech flowed out
everyone and everything
swapped together
and thus a storyteller
was born into this world
one who married
the Gael with the Frank
who listened and spoke to all
the tongues of the Earth
yet never forgot to honour
the pulse, the beat
on her goat-skinned bodhrán
straw-ber-ry straw-ber-ry jigs
wa-ter-mel-on wa-ter-mel-on reels
she danced before she could talk
drummed before she could sing

Snow Crones

Up and down
the midwinter block
small snowflakes
big snowfall
blanketed lawns
a pristine stage
for two crones
who lay together
after midnight
before every home
gesturing bodies
sometimes subtle
sometimes bold
they created
stories and dances
in the cold crystals
so in sparkling
morning light
neighbours followed
the steps
the feelings
of woman-wisdom
old-child abandon
as keen winds
carried laughter
from ancient
invincible
hearts

Ode to an Uncle
i.m. Murray Tyndall

If
as Ai Weiwei has said
Everything is art
everything is politics

then
everything is family
the man at the tiller
of his sailboat, my uncle
John Murray Allan Tyndall
takes us out of Midland
into Georgian Bay waters
we are like congruent triangles
so similar, yet different
both he and I share
myopia and astigmatism
so we can wear
each other's glasses
but we have seldom really
seen each other because
he and my father
were never close
Guy would not forgive
Murray, earnest evangelical
in the Forties and Fifties
telling him he was doomed
to hell-fire damnation
while Murray forgave
but never forgot
my father, covered
in a bearskin rug
growling his fierce way
into his brother's bedroom
like a monster in the night
but here *we* are now
in the new light of day

If family, then also
everything is science
everything is mathematics
for Murray taught high-school
science courses all his life
and we witness the physics
of sailing, the biomechanics
of changing direction
on the starboard tack
we talk hydrodynamics
lake zoology, shoreline botany
we look at the sails
right-angled triangles
curving in space/time
and wonder about
formulae to describe them
and our holy selves

Mind How You Go
i.m. Ron Smith

from the front doorway
you fade into
the star-splashed
rock-scarped night

from Avignon by barge
down the Rhône
to Arles and Agde
the oyster beds and mountains
of sea-salt you savour
local food and wine
the wine, the wine

from a hit at the mat
around all the bases
and back to home
you run and score
then drink "tea" not
from a flask but
a silver service

from the hack
of a curling rink
gliding toward
the hog line
you send your stone
with a finesse of turn
to the house and
on the button

from the Bruce Trail
through rattlesnake cover
your hiking stick
marks the miles
step by step by step

from sheltered anchorage
in Georgian Bay
you sail away with
only the canvas
before the wind
prevailing
all the way
to somewhere

Mind how you go, you say
for you know not
when the going
ends

For All Time Lamenting
for Doug Smith, with thanks to Robin Robertson

Doug played the pipes
in farewell to Ron
his elder brother
on a hillside over-
looking Colpoys Bay
a sad Spring interment
with a bright blue sky
of coming Summer
and a chill wind
of Winter past
the breath-filled bag
sounded the drones
and with his fingers
upon the chanter
he performed *The Flowers
of the Forest*
but was it emotion
made him stumble
in the melody

(During the second war
 Ron pushed Doug's pram
 along Wiarton's rocky shore
 to the rusted iron spiral
 stairs and up the steps
 to the escarpment top
 because it was a boy's life
 and no baby brother
 would slow him down)

This lone rendition
at the gravesite
carried mourners off
while still on Earth
in this valley
where every piper
who plays *The Flowers*
adds a deliberate
mistake to ward off
the bad lucky

Hear That?

I can almost see my son
on the steep trail
from the Rimrock Resort
to the Banff Springs Hotel
from Sulphur Mountain
down to the Bow River
hiking through conifers
that echo with the cries
of Whisky Jack and Raven
spirits at ancient play
atop spiral branches
aloft strong up-draught

He's on alert
for deer and elk
unafraid phantoms
of the parkland
reappear
close to silence
disappear
but for scat
and cloven tracks

I listen to his footfalls
on soft-needle pathway
perceive a strange
whispery sound
over his cellphone
then intake of breath
before he asks

Hear that?
Hear the rain
in the pine trees?

Gordon (Joe)
i.m. Gordon Thede

The first day I knew
cousin Joe had died
from recurrent cancer
I walked to work
along the Thames River
sounds of liquid flowing
around rocks, through snagged branches
in standing waves and whirlpools
brought his voice to mind
celebrating his parents' lives
on their golden anniversary
or telling tales of the power
his grandfather Thede harnessed
on the Sauble River
or portraying the fate of our great-
great-great-grandfather
Ludwig Wideman
and Joe all in costume
an old musket to hand

As I followed the path
beside north river branch
I heard an assailment
of crows over the waters
and turned to see an eagle
forge ahead and away
from its malign tormentors
soaring at ease upstream
even unto the source

Undetermined Significance

Boys, Are You Buzzing?

You're going to lose that group
yes, yes, you're going to lose
that group of limbs
once a smooth unit
like a seasoned band
left leg and foot
stamping out rhythm
in a Cuban-heeled boot
right leg and foot
driving the kick-pedal
bass-drum beat
left arm and hand
hitting an unstable chord
for an unstoppable song
right arm and hand
picking out a riff
ending in a Picardy third
all four members
playing together
and nothing
could touch them
but there's a new disease
sweeping through you
and the break-up starts
at the very marrow
of your aging body
and the men in white
lab coats ask
if you feel the buzz
as the floor gives way
beneath your kit
and all the neurologists
and all the haematologists
can't put the group
back together again

MGUS GUMS SMUG MUGS

What the hell is it?

Look back to root words
Greek and Latin and German
Monoclonal Gammopathy
Undetermined Significance
single shoot blood feeling
not intensive boundary sign made
bone marrow overproduces
Monoclonal Proteins
single shoot primaries
Extra! Extra!
Auto-immune Response
Peripheral Neuropathy
self not serving promise back
to carry nerve feeling

Who for love has it?

Neurologists report
one in sixty thousand
with the flare
of a botanist
finding a rare
two-headed snake
or an archaeologist
Hermes' caduceus

Where does it affect?

As the diseased
apple tree-trunk
appears sound
its pith attacking
the outer limbs
so the arms, the legs
the hands, the feet
buzz and be numb
at the behest
of the body

When did it first strike?

An old ones' illness
often unknown, unfelt
without nerve damage
this particular case
like an early snowfall
heavy, mischievous
uncalled-for blow
unfolded too soon

Why does it appear?

Locked in the spiral
genome of the species
some chromosome
must react off or on
but the carnival wheel
spins around, around past
radiation, toxic gases
black mould, paraquat
et cetera, et cetera
and if it will stop
nobody knows

   How did it happen?

Remember how you played
at the ball and bat
as a little child
with all your friends
and no-one noticed
the lengthening shadows
the sunset behind the trees
everyone else gone home
until time
became late
and night
had fallen

How She Knew Me

She said she
thought I was
American like she was
so outspoken about
winter and work

I removed my clothes
starting with my long
woollen socks until only
long underwear remained

then she proceeded
with the procedure
on the iliac crest
of my pelvis

first, one needle
to anaesthetize
my flesh
another
to anaesthetize
my bone

first, one instrument
to extract
bone marrow fluids
another
to extract
bone marrow cells

and that felt
like someone stirring
my very soul

no pain, no
pain, no pain
only my core
giving it up
for science
for diagnosis

take this, doctor
may it serve you well

I replaced my clothes
over bloodstained
long johns, lastly
my long woollen socks

*

At my follow-up
appointment, results
confirmed MGUS
as my ailment

she said she
had seen me
walking home
from work
day after day

she said she
knew me
by my socks

to Dance

Remember when you first
learned to dance, taught
by your sister and her friend
how to waltz
one two three
aye bee sea
foe fie fee
how to jive
rock 'n' roll
how to do
The Watusi
The Twist
El Dorado for girls
at high school hops
with The Volcanoes

And wouldn't you know
you'd meet and fall in love
with a woman who lived
to tread the sprung floor
hour after hour after hour
fast or slow, close or apart

But just when you began
to learn ballroom dancing
the glide, glide
step step
glide, glide
step step
of the fox trot
the one, two
cha cha cha
it all fell apart
for neuropathic limbs
your balance   off
your timing   off
and your dancing seemed
over forever

Hey, not so fast
rug-cutter
you can still reggae
slow-skanking
one TWO three FOUR
both YOU once MORE

still make love dance
on your elbows and knees

El Dorado

EMG us

every nerve
every limb
diffuse numbness
sensory irregularity

I lay on a lab table
undressed in underwear
and a hospital gown
flimsy almost filmy

with utmost precision
the technician
applied electrodes
pathway by pathway

when she shocked
right median study
I focussed on my left fist
when she shocked
left median study
I focussed on my right fist

she recorded my electromyogram
prolonged terminal latency
reduced conduction velocity
via three levels of current

the first as comical
as a high school frog
temporal dispersion in wave forms

the second as insistent
as a juddering middle leg
responses mildly prolonged

the third as painful
as a torturer's initial jolt
deep peroneal study

and I came to love
her calm but forceful voice
her Mitteleuropean accent

I would have told her
everything

Kappa Lambda

The frat boys
of Kappa Lambda
are throwing an on-going
kegger in their house
my body
they're busy little guys
all dressed down
in sweatshirts
with K Λ on the front
and on the back
either *Anti-MAG*
or *Free Light Chains*

Who knows why
they're all running amok
maybe something oozing
out of the very timbers
of this sexagenarian
makes them sing along
Let's Go Crazy
as they roam
room by room by room
stripping the wiring
cheering every spark
every funny blue arc
as if the aging mansion
were a sideshow funhouse

All except one
Eddie in the corner
with his crib sheet
in his left hand
and his highlighter
in his right
studying for a final
he mouths the points
surely of some significance

Myelin

Myelin-Associated Glycoproteins

Demyelinization

*Antibody synthesis occurs
to produce free light chains*

*Patients with B-cell disorders
host monoclonal immunoglobulin
free light chains*

Abnormal kappa-lambda FLC-ratio

Suddenly the hob-globulin
can resist no longer
throws his notes away
and joins in the fray
screams to the attic

*Just be thankful
we're not at play
in your brain*

Blood Work

The doctors of physick
applied thirsty leeches
to suck away melancholic
humour that one be not
so serious, so cloudy

The Mayan priests
demonstrated the sacred
thorn-knotted cord
drawn through tongue
cheek, glans penis
to splash the altar
to feed the setting god

The mobile blood-bankers
asked whether to withdraw
the red, red, red
from the left arm
or the right arm
for the public good

Nay and nay and nay
for depression will pass
our sun will rise
without offerings
and nobody wants
my *baaad* antibodies
loose in their body

But I do give blood
according to a paper
like a dim sum menu
with careful ticks
next to orders for
protein, bilirubin
immunoglobulins

Vial after vial
after vial fills
up in its turn
takes a label
and clatters
upon a tray

And, glory be
the haematologist
at the cancer clinic
will not ask again of me
this blood work
for six whole months

Farewell Angelika

Always Dr. H___
always the professional
neurologist, yes
but she never hid
her compassion, her regard
all my yearly appointments
at the hospital clinic
up to her retirement
so I say to her
Farewell Angelika
Farewell

She would open
her black case, reveal
all the instruments
to gauge my neuro-
muscular degeneration
– the hand grip dynamometer
when I would fantasize
strength training
while she recorded
left and right
maximums
– the reflex hammer
rapped on wrists
knees and ankles
where not even
Thor's hammer
could have caused
involuntary spasms
– the sensory testing pinwheel
rolled over my pastry limbs
like a dough docker
traced flesh that never
will feel it

– the tuning fork
a one-note vibration
not the twelve tones
of Arnold Schoenberg
applied to toes
(nothing)
applied to heels
(something)
applied to knees
(something more)
– the single pin
pricking my feet
to no effect
– the sensuous feather
raising no response

She never condescended
about my ability
to discover for myself
her academic research
You work in a library
you know how to find it
she never gave false hope
when clinical studies
offered no relief
no cure for MGUS

I am grateful now
to have survived
this long without
myeloma or lymphoma
and be introduced
to her successor
the good Dr. K_____
and I say
Farewell Angelika
Hello Kurt

Tarnished Lining

Sir, on a scale
from 1 to 11
where 1 is the least
and 11 is the worst
what is your pain

Zero, you say

She'll be back
once combined general
and local anaesthesia
have had more time
to wear off after
orthopaedic surgery

Your surgeon, at first
loth to operate
on your broken fibula
due to your neuropathy
You won't be able to tell
if something goes wrong
ordered a cast worthy
of royal Egyptian mummification
then changed his professional mind
when x-rays revealed
your bone still unknitted
thus the plate, the screws
the scar, that nurse
again *On a scale*
from 1 to 11
what is your pain

Less than zero

Your very own
silver lining, huh
and with two unfilled
prescriptions you received

for Percocet you could
have made a killing
on the street
or, perhaps, more likely
caused a death

But all the complications
after breaking your ankle
had a simple cause
you thought you'd suffered
only a sprain on the ice
and walked a kilometre
back to your office
when nothing hurt

So heigh-ho, heigh-ho
it's a tarnished lining
everywhere you go now
Dopey

FX-rays

My doctors required
a full-body X-ray
in their quest
for evidence
of bone cancer
they ordered multiple
views from my carpals
to my tarsals
every rib
every vertebra
frontal skull
parietal skull
temporal skull
occipital skull

Consider all the X-rays
during my lifetime
that body scan
dental records
ankle plate and screws
my sorry lungs

How many rads
have I received
how many short waves
how many sub-
atomic bombardments

How many images
could one make
from the passage
of particles

Imagine all the pictures
as photo collage, as animation
my dry bones going
to rise again
as entertainment
as art
for surely the technician
was an artist
of the electron tube
posing my body
for the session
like a life model

Now I wish
I had been
naked

Blet

Even at rest
my legs are not
completely still
I can see
the calves roiling
like sacks
of serpents
even at rest
the motor nerves
may fire in pain-
ful spikes

The first I felt
something grown
wrong with my limbs
I was climbing the path
to Blackfriars Bridge
my arms and legs
electrically buzzing
with no cardio-
vascular stress

If I were a piece
of ripened fruit
a pear perchance
you could not tell
from my sweet skin
that I am sleepy
at the core
that I suffer
a blet
so if you wish
to eat of me
do not bite
for all love
too deep

Praesagia mortis

Far across a fen dotted
with Summer's last flowers
Grass of Parnassus
Fringed Gentian
Nodding Ladies' Tresses
(white and blue dwarfs
 of a marshy heaven)
I hear aspens rustling
in a north wind
speak of passing
away, again, away

A ruddy fox
skirts the yard
dismisses my presence
no threat, my neuro-
pathetic legs
no match, his four-
pawed elegance
with brief beauty
on his side

A Chickadee flits
from thick cedars
to sundial engraved
Time will tell
just a quarter rest
before she dives
to my sandalled toes
for already I may
harbour insects

Far across the fen still
I hear the north wind
in the trembling aspens

O the beautiful
omens of death

Creative Compensation

Feels like a forced trek
in a desert land
when it's only me
up from a river path
onto a hot sidewalk
off to see a movie
but my neuro-degrading
legs are giving out
in the summer heat
as I march – by the left

hup
        two
three
        four
hup
        two
three
        four

and even my swinging arms
cannot keep me from tottering
like a novice stilt-walker
caught in variable winds

Then I have a vision
of the holy crone
Margaret Avison
slowly approaching
the Griffin Prize podium
before she announced
This is just ridiculous
and I remember she said
in some interview
Walk in steps
of five or seven
so I try it out
five by five

        right
left
        right
left
        right

left
        right
left
        right
left

and, lo, it works
what my neurologist calls
creative compensation
for fraying autonomics

Hey, my legs
and my poetics

we
        can
work
        it
out

        we
can
        work
it
        out

Undetermined Significance

Bad news, good news

Blood proteins persist
the chance of cancer rises
one per cent per year
the deathly slope towards
myeloma or lymphoma
slowly, slowly proceeds
so my neurologist sees me
every two years rather than
every twelve months
and my haematologist
checks me every year
not every six months

More and more I lose it
out loud or inside my head
my fucking feet
my fucking arms and legs
my fucking fingers
now I can no longer run
will never leap from rock to
rock on any liminal shore
nor throw a baseball right to you
nor feel my belovèd's skin
with my own hands

Oh, but I can
walk and walk and walk
still swim and dive
still dance a few steps
still kiss

So, yes, the ailment
has undetermined significance
like the dream I recall
leaving a Raj-era restaurant
to catch the Express
to the Roof of the World

carrying only
an empty backpack
an empty wallet

Go Ahead John

Tell you what

go to your shelves
pull out that album
you bought in 1974
MILES
DAVIS
BIG
FUN
put on vinyl side three
and listen to your own
neuromuscular disorder

DeJohnette's drumming
switches back and forth
left to right to left
to right to left to right
mimicking your arms swinging
so you do not fall on
dangerous stair-steps

Macero the producer
engineered that effect
and, oh, what he did
to McLaughlin's electric
guitar, a solo already
angry blasting crazy
he toggled off
like a vague memory
picked up by ambient mics
he toggled on
like a hard agony
in and out
over and over
corrosive
c rros ve
c rr s v

Sound so compelling
you imagine yourself
in New York City
at the 30th Street Studio
musicians call
The Church

You look up
and through the glass
to the control room

Over the talk-back speaker
you hear The Voice
command

Go ahead, John

Play

Listen

Everything I Know
about Library Science
I Learned from
The Kenny Burrell Quartet

We funky librarians
flee Windsor workshops
to Baker's Keyboard Lounge
The World's Oldest Premier Jazz Venue
hallowed ground on Livernois
where the great ones

     sing

   play

 burn

Where tonight four musicians
tap the electric life-source
in series, in parallel

quartet

  trio

    duo

      solo

man
rolls rhythm sticks
to man
plucks pizzicato strings
to man
chords chromatic keys
to man
lights liquid fires

The text may be Ellington
all joyous black tuxedo style
or happy calypso birthday jazz
or unwritten songstory
out of the airy shadows
the wine sweat smoky time
taken to throw a glancing smile

but we learn our lesson
keep our ear-won memory
our reward in jazz haven

The Kenny Burrell Quartet
gives us pure knowledge

now we bring it home
to discover wisdom

The Archer and the Ugly Tourist
for Linda Bone

She is an archer
skilled at sighting
and hitting targets
whether solo hunt
or fierce competition
she bends the bow
one with the mark
and the release
but in hospital
with her eldest son
she gets the word
mastectomy
and she's thinking
what he's thinking
she will become
an Amazon
able to draw
the bowstring
unimpeded

although arrows
will not suffice
to kill the cancer
travelling inside

Here's how she sees *it*

She's relaxing
on a palm-shaded beach
wearing her new
blue bathing suit
when she spies him

as ugly a tourist
as ever was
loudly obnoxious
complaining about
everything
appearing and vanishing
from the shoreline
the restaurant
the nightspot
and though she'd like
to try her luck
at archery
instead she heeds
the faint tremors
beneath the sands
and joins the rest
of the tribe quietly
moving to higher ground
turning her back
on the brute because
this isn't Florida
it's an island
near Malaysia
and a tsunami
is approaching
to sweep him
away

Tattered

When I heard that
retired government
publications librarian
Maureen Elizabeth Ryan
had died from her cancer
I was still drying myself
with the bath towels
she gave my wife and me
on our wedding day
over three decades ago
the green terry cloth
almost as bright and plush
as the day she bought the set
at long-gone Eaton's store
although the seams have frayed
and I trim the trailing threads
although the narrow end-panels
have fallen away forever
there is enough pile left
to soak up my tears

I am ever sentimental
I am yet using, washing
drying a towel my parents
received for their wedding
at the war's end and
as I cherish their memory
so I cherish Maureen's

my heart both tattered
and strong

Zsuzsánna is in Love Forever

Zsuzsi fell in love
with a voice broadcast
on Hungarian state radio
not first secretary János Kádár
of the Socialist Workers' Party
He who is not against us
is with us
and welcomed by us
not prime minister Gyula Kállai
newly sworn in that Summer of 1965
but a foreign voice
from the land of the Scots
from the city of Glasgow
a strummer, a singer
of the colours of sky
and a lover's hair
whose complaint
that war dragged on
sidestepped the censors

When Zsuzsi came to Canada
she embraced songs
she'd never heard before
in that soft vibrato
about Goodge Street
South Kensington
Hampstead Heath
and they spoke her heart
and she hummed her joy

Zsuzsánna szereti Donovant mindörökke

Sit Back and Listen
i.m. MacLean Jamieson

Stan writes
that Mac has died
and my memories
thirty-five years ago
become clear

we share whisky
at the droogy launch
of my book of Howlcat
savour the glens
in the midst of
punky Ramones and
lurid Riefenstahl

Mac jaunty saunters
down Queens Ave
with his furled umbrella
ready for thunder-rains
upon this lesser London

his stubborn folly – trying
to publish books and journals
sans government money
in an age of postal
strikes and stoppage
and no orders come

my dinner evening
with the Jamiesons
Mac urges me to buy
albums by Nick Drake
and then retires to
his music room
leaving jill and me
to talk Philip K. Dick
the real and the paranoid
until we hear the piano
and jill says *Mac*
is playing Scriabin
Sit back and listen

Only a Dream Camino
for David Murphy

I arrive late
at the *albergue*
in a small city
on the pilgrim's way
to Santiago de Compostela
a volunteer tut-tuts
over my muddy shoes
as we approach
the dining room
where I take
the last seat
across from Thomas
who asks *So
is this the end
for you?*
I doubt it, I reply
as a man stands up
with the question
*How many of you
saw the Cross today?*
a flurry of hands
a scatter of answers
*Atop a village church
At a roadside shrine
On a golden chain
around the neck
of the woman from Galway*
and when he points to me

I announce *I see it*
everywhere, in everything
vapour trails across the sky
medieval masonry
each crossroad
here, in the ceiling panels
the flooring tiles
window panes

I rise out of my chair
spread my arms out wide

in everyone I meet

Raven Plays the Mountain
for Cornelia Hoogland

At the foot of Sulphur Mountain
people at Banff frolic in the fume
of frothing hot springs
they soak and burn away
the ache of ski trails
and too much fine spirit
micro-brew and pinot noir
golden weed and white, white blow
only a few ages set free
from the primeval clam-shell
and the havoc runs
amok around the clock
the beautiful sad ones
let their hair hang down
before they slip into the scald

Raven has flown to this peak
and faced the steady winds
since land first dried
and rose to icy heights
he has spread wings, fanned tail
and tumbled backwards
over the summit, joyous
in this cacophonous comedy
soared above evergreens
to play the mountain
again and again
to make the snow fall
and the water flow
to his call

The First Time Alice Munro Asked Me a Question

And then smiling she appeared
in the library lineup
at the information desk
and while I wondered where
were her pencils, her fountain pen
why is she not writing
she asked me for help
with the pronunciation
of a native name
Search as I might
all I could do was suggest
equal stress on every syllable
Me - Ne - Se - Teung
and then smiling she disappeared

Later that night I stood in line
behind her for the cinema
she remembered me but
did she hear my thought

*Come back, Alice, come
back and ask me another*

Take Up What You Hear
for R.E.M.

Back then
the singer still
had hair
the drummer, well
he was a drummer
not a farmer
and all four
guitar and bass, too
toured out of a van
drove to the hall
just the opening act
the day before
their first album
appeared in stores
but the band, talk
about passion, performed
louder, more fierce
than headliners
with twice the number
their only light show
two spots on the sides
throwing shadows
on both concert walls
doubling the players, so
everyone's eyes danced
back and forth
in rapid movement
twinned with ears
in chiming, chiming
need to *take*
a souvenir

In the Wheelhouse
for Craig Simpson

Stepping up to the plate I heard
through our players' bravado
about being tough out there
and batting like I can
clear as a skipper's call
from his pilothouse *John*
you are the winning run
I nodded to you once, ignored
the first slow-pitches
inside and outside balls
a lousy strike that kissed
a corner of the mat
It's got to be
in the wheelhouse
you spoke to my heart
and the next high arc
met the best path of my left-
hand roundhouse swing

and that softball
soared over fielders
hungry for an out
so I steamed
around the bases
like a lean locomotive
only to be stopped by you
for a stand-up triple
just short of the homer you knew
I couldn't have safely made

and I knew it, too
I was already
awaiting your command
at the tag-up hit

Go!

Two Paths
for Catherine Morrisey

Ray hikes in boots	Cath barefootin' treads
along Alaskan trail	through Jasper landscape
wooded rough blaze	trees a thousand greens
to a sluice-site creek	to a cobalt lake
his claim, his stake	her favourite scene
where he'll pan for gold	where she'll memorize golds
seek nuggets or dust	ochres and umbers
when his neck bristles	when her eyes dart left-right
as if a rival prospector	at what looks different
seeks the same El Dorado	in the Edenic forest
he glances behind	she thinks she sees
at a distant shadow	a stump with ears
a grizzly tracker	no, a mountain lion
ursine predator	no, two mountain lions
he quickens pace	she freezes still
his rifle ready	under close regard
he glances again	she poses awhile
the bear now gone	for the tawny pair
he sweats every bend	too inquisitive to attack
expects an ambush	before she passes by
that never comes	she says *Meow*

Himselven (ghazal)

All those birds by his snoring he'd awoken himselven
retaliated with song and have woken himselven

Like many who have felt but a shell of their youthful selves
here on this world stage he's sometimes a token himselven

In a Greek restaurant amid a myriad poets
with retsina-tangy voice he has spoken himselven

As warm as wool and as soft as silk and as light as lace
this woman's love has rested in a cloak on himselven

If only both his feet had slid on that snow-hidden patch
of black and smooth ice he would not have broken himselven

Off balance and clumsy like a horse with the blind staggers
his old-man's body slyly tells a joke on himselven

Whether the hue has shone berserker red or housebound gray
his beardy bristles have always bespoken himselven

Using ancient letters we solemnly inherited
he bequeaths his friends these lines that betoken himselven

Watch the Rivervalley Man float graciously by and by
in a boat built from woods piney and oaken himselven

Stars, the Stars

I am walking after dark
the road to Lonely Island
in high summer
where I have strolled
and swum all my life
I remove my glasses
and from every cottage
every light glows
like a faceted gem
with my lenses replaced
a campfire dances
from the earth to the air
the constellations arc
along the galaxy's rim
now the road curves
in a causeway, imagine
an Aztec city
wildflowers lining the path
I enter the island
follow the way clockwise
to the north boat-launch
climb down to a wooden dock
and lie on my back
head aligned with Polaris
with my eyes closed
I can hear young lovers
nightswimming off Whisky Island
voices and splashes and silence
and with my eyes open
see only celestial drift
for this dock floats
upon the waters
and suspends me
in stars, the stars

Moniker, Handle, Tag

When I get bolder
in the near, near future
maybe just possibly
I might become
an infamous graffitist
hoodied and flying
around this dull city
hauling out the spray-paint
to disfigure buildings
and brutal infrastructure
with my personal mark

always in black letters
always a step ahead
of the pretty little police
coming so close to discovery
I doff my sweat-shirt
to throw them off
then change things up
for phase two
with a stencil
of the highway sign

defacing this town
but never showing up
on any security camera
putting those other
taggers to shame
and doing it all
by next October
when I'm sixty-four

Hoo!

Haunt

I am haunting the living-
room window of the house
where I grew up a lanky teen
elbows upon meeting rails
head against sash bar
as though leaning on the Cross
passersby and residents
see me at twilit dawn
and dusk staring out
upon a cyclone-cracked
horse-chestnut tree
Spring's frothy flowers
Autumn's prickly pericarps
a tree no longer there

I am haunting the bedroom
window as a small child
arms resting on the sill
of a Summer's night
curtains blowing inward
obliques of car-light caressing
my eyes, my hair, my skin
arms resting on the sill
of a Winter's day
through a square pane
my gaze upon a perfect circle
maple branches form
across the snowy street
a ring only visible
at this very window
like a constellation
only we on Earth perceive
a great roundel within
a tree no longer there

This house my haunt
while I live herein
and I the haunt
now no longer here

Acknowledgements

"*Boys, Are You Buzzing?*" first appeared in *Window Fishing: The Night We Caught Beatlemania* (Hidden Brook Press, 2013), edited by John B. Lee.

"Everything I Know about Library Science I Learned from The Kenny Burrell Quartet" first appeared in *Canadian Author*. I dedicate it to Elizabeth Mantz (who was there that night on her birthday) and Christy and Dan Sich (who found it and read it for my retirement party).

"Raven Plays the Mountain" first appeared on Cornelia Hoogland's blog *Crow*: https://crow2011.wordpress.com/blog/

"The First Time Alice Munro Asked Me a Question" first appeared in *The Windsor Review*.

My thanks to:

the following doctors for professional care: Pellar, Leaf, Hahn, Minuk, Lawendy, Kimpinski, Louzada, and Takahashi;

Michael-John Idzerda for the cover image;

Tom Adam for "little snow, big snow" and Wayne Knott for "the blind staggers";

Richard (Tai) Grove and all at Hidden Brook Press;

the group in London, Ontario and my friend and editor, John B. Lee.

John Tyndall lives in London, Ontario with his wife, Diane Halpin. He worked over four decades at The D.B. Weldon Library at Western University, helping generations of students discover and document information for their academic research. His previous books include *The Fee for Exaltation* (Black Moss, 2007) and *Free Rein* (Black Moss, 2001). His poems have also appeared in many anthologies, such as *Translating Horses: The Line, The Thread, The Underside* (Baseline, 2015), edited by Jessica Hiemstra and Gillian Sze, and the journals *The Windsor Review* and *The Fiddlehead*. This year of 2020 marks the fiftieth anniversary of his first meeting with John B. Lee in an introductory class to English Literature at Western.

www.ingramcontent.com/pod-product-compliance
Lightning Source LLC
Chambersburg PA
CBHW020545080526
44583CB00013B/1002